Easy Halloween Projects

you can paint

By Sugar Brushes,
Margaret Wilson & Robyn Thomas

N

NORTH LIGHT BOOKS

CINCINNATI, OHIO
www.artistsnetwork.com

Dedications

It is with a loving and humble heart that I dedicate this book to my husband, Ronnie. No matter what, he has always been supportive and encouraging. Without his help and understanding I would never have had the opportunities to design and teach. And, also, to all of the wonderful students who encourage and take classes. I thank you from the bottom of my heart.

—Margaret Wilson

I would like to dedicate this book to my family: my son Adam, my best critic, will truthfully tell me it is bad and give suggestions to make it better; my oldest son, Brandon, who always knew when I needed help and would entertain and watch over the younger kids so I could work; my twin daughters, Meghan and Sarah, who think everything I do is wonderful and take great pleasure in telling people I'm an artist; and to my greatest supporter, my husband, Michael. Without your love and dedication I wouldn't have been able to do this. Love to you all.

—Robyn Thomas

Easy Halloween Projects You Can Paint. Copyright © 2003 by Margaret Wilson and Robyn Thomas. Manufactured in Singapore. All rights reserved. The patterns and drawings in the book are for personal use of reader. By permission of the author and publisher, they may be either hand-traced or photocopied to make single copies, but under no circumstances may they be resold or republished. It is permissible for the purchaser to make the projects contained herein and sell them at fairs, bazaars and craft shows. No other part of this book may be reproduced in any form or by any electronic or mechanical means including information storage and retrieval systems without permission in writing from the publisher, expect by a reviewer, who may quote a brief passage in review. Published by North Light Books, an imprint of F&W Publications, Inc., 4700 E. Galbraith Rd., Cincinnati, Ohio 45236. (800) 289-0963. First edition.

07 06 05 04 03   5 4 3 2 1

Library of Congress Cataloging-in-Publication Data
Wilson, Margaret
   Easy Halloween projects you can paint / by Sugar Brushes, Margaret Wilson & Robyn Thomas.
      p. cm.
   Includes Index.
   ISBN 1-58180-382-6
   1. Halloween decorations. 2. Acrylic Painting. I. Thomas, Robyn, II. Title.

   TT900.H32 W557 2003
      745.594'1646--dc21   200237957

Editors: Catherine Cochran and David Oeters
Production Coordinator: Michelle Ruberg
Designer: Joanna Detz
Page Layout Artist: Kathy Bergstrom
Photographers: Christine Polomsky and Tim Grondin

METRIC CONVERSION CHART

TO CONVERT	TO	MULTIPLY BY
Inches	Centimeters	2.54
Centimeters	Inches	0.4
Feet	Centimeters	30.5
Centimeters	Feet	0.03
Yards	Meters	0.9
Meters	Yards	1.1
Sq. Inches	Sq. Centimeters	6.45
Sq. Centimeters	Sq. Inches	0.16
Sq. Feet	Sq. Meters	0.09
Sq. Meters	Sq. Feet	10.8
Sq. Yards	Sq. Meters	0.8
Sq. Meters	Sq. Yards	1.2
Pounds	Kilograms	0.45
Kilograms	Pounds	2.2
Ounces	Grams	28.4
Grams	Ounces	0.04

About the Authors

Margaret Wilson has always had a love for art. While still teaching elementary school, she signed up for a decorative painting class during the summer break. This was all she needed to become completely hooked. She began teaching painting at home in the evening while still teaching school during the day. After retiring from teaching in West Carrollton, Ohio, she moved with her husband to Wall Lake near Delton, Michigan. Here she helped organize the Michigan Grapevine Decorative Artist chapter in Kalamazoo and met Robyn Thomas.

Robyn Thomas has been painting for 15 years. She started painting seriously when her daughters were just babies. She needed something to satisfy her creative side, but it had to be fast. Raising four children, the last two being twins, didn't leave a lot of time to finish a project. With painting she could create something beautiful without spending months or days to complete it. When her daughters started school she began to travel teach.

At about the same time, Margaret Wilson, another member of her local painting chapter, also started travel teaching. They decided to travel and room together to share expenses. In the process, they became good friends and in 1995 started the designing team Sugar Brushes. Together they have developed hundreds of pattern packets and co-authored three books. You can see them at several of the larger decorative painting conventions, manning their booth and teaching classes.

Acknowledgments

We would like to acknowledge and thank our many friends at North Light Books, including our editor, Catherine Cochran, for all the calls, e-mails and updates she gave us so we remained in touch with our book through its long process; and our photographer, Christine Polomsky, who made every shot look wonderful while making us feel totally at home.

Special thank yous to Tricia Waddell for making this book a reality, and last, but certainly not least, to Sally Finnegan and her staff. Without their promotion and expertise we would not be successful.

We would also like to acknowledge our good friends and mentors, Judy Diephouse and Lynne Deptula. Without these two wonderful ladies we would not be where we are today. Thank you.

Table of Contents

Introduction

Welcome and thank you for joining us.

Halloween is one of our favorite holidays, second only to Christmas. It allows you to be very creative, whether you're trying to find the perfect costume or planning that special get-together.

Show your guests they are special by sending them a handmade Ghostly Invitation. Greet them as they come up the driveway with a friendly Scarecrow Yard Sign or perhaps a Spooky Wreath. Once you have them inside, dazzle them with your table. They will love to see the glow from your Black Cat Candle, and the Candy Corn Dishes are sure to be a hit. Then, at the end of your party, send them home with a hand-painted Refrigerator Magnet. They will be anticipating next year's party every time they look at it.

We hope you have had an opportunity to check out our first book, *Easy Christmas Projects You Can Paint.* Like our first book, we have chosen a variety of surfaces that are easy to find or easily substituted. We've kept the projects simple so you can quickly paint several pieces to decorate your home or perhaps to sell at your fall craft shows.

Don't worry if you've never picked up a brush before. In this book we'll teach you basic painting techniques. We will also show you the proper way to prepare surfaces so you will be able to paint on just about anything.

We hope you enjoy painting the projects as much as we enjoyed creating them for you. Happy painting!

Supplies

Before starting your project, be sure you have all the necessary supplies. The following pages will show you what you need to complete the projects in this book. These supplies are readily available at your nearby arts and crafts stores. Before you know it, you will have some awesome Halloween projects to admire.

BRUSHES

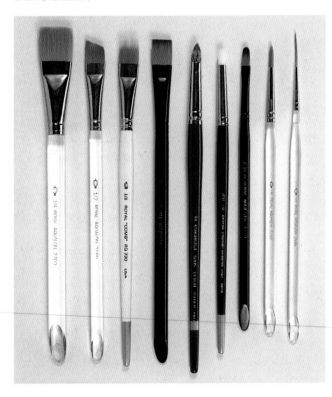

Brushes pictured left to right: glaze, angle, comb, flat, sable, scrubber, filbert, round, and liner brushes.

Brushes are the most important piece of equipment for the painter. Keep them in good condition by cleaning them well after each use. In this book we used brushes by Royal & Langnickle. A beginner needs a minimum of three basic brushes: a flat or angle, a round, and a liner. As you gain experience painting, you will find that adding specialty brushes makes the painting go much more quickly. Each brush has a particular function. Eventually, you will develop a certain "feel" to achieve a particular look, and this feel will help you choose the appropriate brush. As you begin to paint the various projects in this book, please note the types of brushes we recommend.

Angle Brush: a brush cut on an angle. It helps the beginner with floating color.

Comb Brush: sometimes called a rake brush, the bristles are cut into various lengths. Usually used to do hair, fur or grass. Use a very light touch and thinned paint.

Deerfoot Brush: also called a stippling brush, this round brush is cut on an angle. Sometimes a worn, old brush can be used to stipple. Usually used to do foliage, highlighting or shading.

Filbert Brush: a brush with the bristles rounded so it looks like an upside-down U. Sometimes it's called a cat's tongue. Great for making leaves, flower petals or anything with a rounded edge.

Flat Brush: a staple item for craft painters and decorative artists. It's used for basecoating and for floating color.

Glaze Brush: a soft bristle brush used to finish pieces with varnish or glaze.

Liner Brush: a basic brush available in many lengths and sizes. A rule of thumb is that the longer the bristle, the less the control. We used medium-length bristles in this book.

Round Brush: a necessary brush used for basic strokes, daisy petals and leaves.

Sable Brush: a round brush made of natural hairs. It's great for stippling.

Scrubber Brush: a round fabric brush with stiff white nylon bristles.

Sponge Brush: a foam brush used to basecoat large surfaces.

ADDITIONAL SUPPLIES

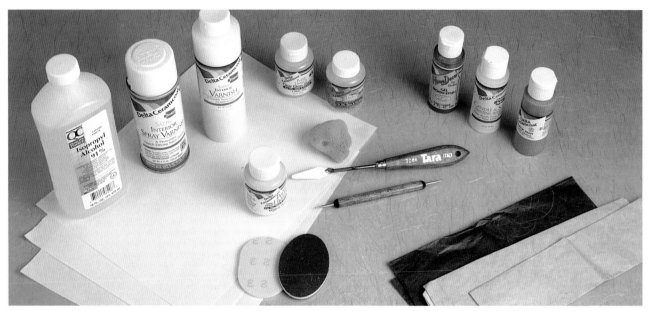

Supplies pictured clockwise, starting from lower left: tracing paper, rubbing alcohol, spray varnish, brush-on varnish, clear gloss glaze, air-dry enamel paint, fruit gel stain, candle and soap painitng medium, acrylic paint, graphite paper, sanding disks, stylus, palette knife, sea sponge.

Acrylic Paint: is a water-based paint. There are a variety of brands available at craft stores. We used Delta Ceramcoat on all of the projects in this book.

Air-Dry Enamel Paint: is a group of specialty paints for non-porous surfaces such as tile, glass and glazed ceramics—surfaces on which you cannot use acrylic paint. We use Delta's Air-Dry PermEnamels.

Brush-on Varnish: is a water-based varnish used to protect finished wood projects. Interior and exterior varnishes are available.

Candle and Soap Painting Medium: is used with acrylic paints to allow paint to adhere to a slick surface, such as candles or soap. Follow the manufacturer's directions.

Clear Gloss Glaze: acts as a varnish to seal the PermEnamels.

Gel Wood Stain: is a thick water-based stain used to prepare surfaces for painting. It's usually applied with a sponge.

Graphite Paper: transfers patterns to the painting surface. When transferring a pattern to a light surface, use the dark graphite. When transferring a pattern to a dark surface, use the light graphite.

Palette Knife: is a flexible blade used to mix paints.

Palette Paper: is an inexpensive and disposable waxed paper designed to hold your paints.

Rubbing Alcohol: is used to prepare candles for painting.

Sandpaper: is used to smooth surfaces for painting.

Sea Sponge: is a natural sponge used to add dimension and texture when painting.

Spray Varnish: is a water-based varnish used to prepare surfaces like plastic for painting. We use a satin interior spray varnish. To finish a project, you might need to use three to four coats.

Stylus: is used to transfer patterns, make dots and, in this book, to make stars. Use the stylus to transfer patterns without marks, so the pattern can be used over and over.

Surface Conditioner: prepares nonporous surfaces so paint adheres. It is used with Delta's Air-Dry PermEnamels.

Basic Painting Techniques

Now that you have all of your materials gathered together, it's time to review or learn a few basic brushstrokes. The following techniques are a general overview for the brushstrokes used in all the projects.

Loading the Brush

A flat is most commonly used for basecoating. The size of the brush is determined by the amount of area you need to cover. To get the best coverage and the most out of your brushes, load the paint properly.

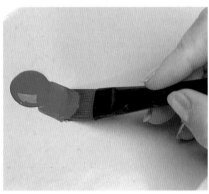

To load the brush to basecoat, first dip the brush into clean water and blot on a paper towel. Next, dip both sides of the brush into the paint puddle. Do not go more than halfway up the bristles of the brush. Work the brush back and forth on a palette until the paint blends with the water in the brush. You are now ready to basecoat.

Making a Wash

A wash of color is often used to tint an area of a design. This diluted value of color is transparent and gives a glossy look.

Dip your flat brush in water, and pull a little paint from the edge of your paint puddle. Work the water with this paint to make a puddle of colored water. Rinse and blot the brush, and then load your brush with the wash.

Loading a Liner

Use a liner brush when painting thin lines, small details or letters. The size of the liner helps determine the size of the line.

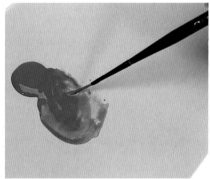

To load your liner brush, dip it in clean water and blot very gently. Use more water with the liner than with other brushes. Thin the paint with water until it has the consistency of ink. Dip the brush into the thinned paint and roll the tip of the liner on the palette away from the paint to form a point, making sure there are no stray hairs. The amount of pressure you use on the brushstroke will help determine the width of the line.

Floating Color

Floating color is a fundamental technique for craft painters requiring a side- or corner-load application of paint. To side-load your brush; apply paint to one corner of the brush letting the color soften and diffuse out to the other side.

This technique allows you to add dimension to your painting. Floating with a darker color than your basecoat is called shading; floating with a lighter color is highlighting.

Corner-Load Float

One Use a flat or angle brush for floating. Make sure your brush is still in good condition with a nice sharp edge to the bristles. Dip it in clean water and blot. Next, holding the brush in a vertical position, dip a corner into the paint. Do not go over one-third the distance across the brush with the paint.

Two Using pressure, blend the paint on the palette. Stay in the same spot on the palette while blending. This will keep the brush filled with paint and prevent you from painting the palette. Work and blend the color into the brush 10 to 12 times before using.

Back-to-Back Float

A back-to-back float is achieved by floating the color, then flipping the brush over so the next float is back-to-back with the first one. Be careful not to butt the two floats. Instead, slightly overlap each to eliminate a hard line in the middle. This technique adds highlights in the center of a design and gives the project dimension.

Scrubbing

This technique, also known as drybrushing, is used to softly highlight an area or add blush color to a cheek.

One To load the fabric scrubber brush for scrubbing, make sure the brush is dry, then dip the brush into the paint.

Two Using a dry paper towel, scrub the brush until almost all of the paint has been removed.

Three With a firm but gentle circular motion, scrub the brush on the surface. Scrub lightly until you have determined the amount of paint still in the brush. Apply more pressure as you continue.

Stippling

This technique adds color and texture. For instance, it's excellent for painting snow on trees.

One Loading the brush for stippling is very much like loading the brush for scrubbing, except that you use a sable or old, worn brush instead of the scrubber. After loading, tap the brush onto a paper towel to eliminate any blobs.

Two To stipple, simply tap the brush up and down in a vertical position. The amount of pressure applied to the brush will determine the amount of paint transferred to the surface.

Sponging

This technique is used when a quick and mottled look is needed. The amount of color can be varied depending on the amount of water in the sponge. The type of sponge (small holes or large holes) will also affect the final result.

One Dip the sponge into clean water and squeeze until just damp. Pick up paint from the edge of the paint puddle with the damp sponge. Tap the sponge onto a paper towel to eliminate any excess.

Two When sponging, use a random approach. Twist and turn the sponge in your hand so no pattern appears.

C-Stroke

This brushstroke refers to the direction your side-loaded brush takes. You actually form a C. This stroke is useful when painting curly hair or adding a highlight or shadow.

One With a side-load application of color, start on the sharp edge of the bristles, which is known as the chisel edge of the brush.

Two Apply pressure to draw the letter C.

Three Release pressure to return to the chisel edge and complete the C-stroke.

One-Stroke Leaf

This brushstroke is a simple way to paint a basic leaf without shading or highlighting.

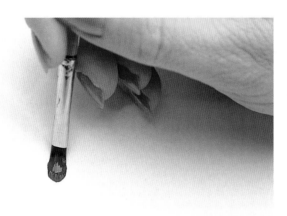

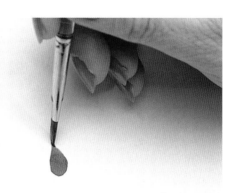

One Load your filbert brush with paint. Apply pressure while the brush is flat.

Two Release pressure as you turn to the chisel edge.

Comma Stroke

This decorative stroke can be done with a liner or a round brush. Comma strokes are perfect for painting facial feature details and highlights.

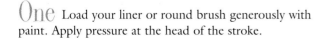

One Load your liner or round brush generously with paint. Apply pressure at the head of the stroke.

Two Release pressure to paint the tail of the stroke.

Preparing Surfaces

In this book, we paint with a variety of surfaces. Before you begin painting, properly prepare the surface so the paint adheres.

Candle

Clean the candle with rubbing alcohol. Let dry for one hour. Do not touch the area where the painting will be. Mix acrylic paint with an equal amount of candle and soap painting medium. You are now ready to paint.

Glass

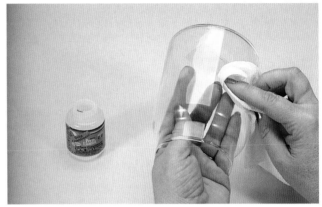

Wash and dry the glass. With the surface conditioner and a paper towel, wipe the area to be painted. Let dry. Be careful not to handle the area to be painted. You are now ready to paint.

Plastic

Wash and dry the plastic so it's free of any dirt or grease. Let dry. Spray with Delta's satin spray varnish and let dry. You are now ready to paint.

Wood

Wood needs to be smooth for easy painting. If necessary, sand with a medium- or fine-grain sandpaper and wipe clean. Next, seal the wood with a sealer or water-based varnish. Let dry. Check if the grain of the wood has been raised. If so, gently resand and wipe clean. You are now ready to paint.

Black cat Candle

What's more fun at Halloween than candles? Whether they're lighting the inside of your favorite pumpkin or casting an eerie glow in a secluded window, candles set the stage. This little candle can do just that—and no one will be afraid of this scaredy cat. So gather some fall leaves and candy, place them around the base and enjoy.

Supplies

6" (15cm) orange pillar candle

candle and soap painting medium

rubbing alcohol

soft cloth

black and white graphite paper

stylus

¾"(1.9cm) Scotch Magic tape

Brushes

no. 1 liner

no. 2 liner

10/0 liner

no. 4 filbert

no. 4 flat

no. 8 flat

½-inch (13mm) flat

Delta Ceramcoat Acrylic Paints

Black

Opaque Yellow

Quaker Grey

Poppy Orange

White

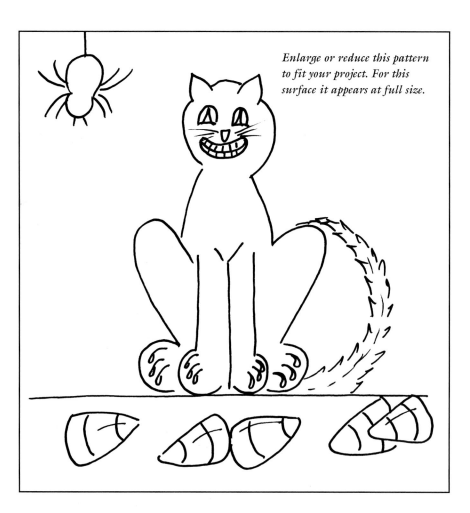

Enlarge or reduce this pattern to fit your project. For this surface it appears at full size.

Prepare the Candle

Clean the candle with a soft cloth and rubbing alcohol according to the directions on the candle and soap painting medium bottle. Tape off 1" (2.5cm) at the bottom of the candle. Mix the candle medium with Black paint and basecoat the bottom of the candle with your ½-inch (13mm) flat brush. Transfer the pattern with black graphite paper. Basecoat the spider and the cat with Black and a ½-inch (13mm) flat brush.

2 | Add the Features

Using Opaque Yellow and a no. 2 liner brush, basecoat the eyes and nose. Stroke in the claws with Opaque Yellow.

3 | Add Details

With a no. 1 liner, define the cat legs with Quaker Grey. Add whiskers and eyelashes. Using your no. 4 flat, place a small float of Quaker Grey just inside the ears. Add the pupils to the eyes with Black and the 10/0 liner.

4 | Finish Mouth and Eyes

With White and a no. 1 liner, add the cat's mouth. Using the 10/0 liner, paint White dots in the eyes at the 2 o'clock position. Outline the lips with your no. 1 liner and Opaque Yellow.

5 Basecoat the Candy Corn

Transfer the candy corn pattern with white graphite paper and basecoat each with White and your no. 4 filbert brush. Add a stripe of Opaque Yellow at the top of each kernel with your no. 4 filbert. With your no. 4 flat, add a stripe of Poppy Orange to the center of each kernel. Using your no. 8 flat and Poppy Orange, float shading on the bottom of each piece and between the two that overlap.

6 Highlight the Candy Corn

Add a shine line to each piece of candy corn with White and your no. 1 liner.

If you like, brush over the candle with candle and soap medium for a final finish.

18

Flying Witch Candle

This flying silhouette against the harvest moon won't scare anyone. But she will make a great addition to the mood of the evening with her wick aglow. This fun candle is easy to do and will harmonize with the other Halloween accessories.

First, prepare the candle by cleaning it with rubbing alcohol, and let it stand about an hour. Place three puddles of paint onto your palette: Mello Yellow, Opaque Yellow and Crocus Yellow. Mix the colors with soap and candle painting medium according to the directions on the bottle. With your sea sponge, pick up all three colors. Sponge onto the candle, covering it completely. Let dry. Transfer the pattern from page 68 and use the no. 8 flat to basecoat the silhouette with black. Use the no. 1 liner for the broom. Dip your stylus in White to paint the stars, pulling the points of the stars with the stylus.

Supplies
candle
rubbing alcohol
soap and candle painting medium
sea sponge
black graphite paper
stylus

Brushes
no. 1 liner
no. 8 flat

Delta Ceramcoat Acrylic Paints
Black
Crocus Yellow
Mello Yellow
Opaque Yellow
White

Candy Corn Dish

Y ou just finished making those yummy cupcakes, and now you need the perfect plate to put them on. You'll reach for this one every time. The candy corn is so bright and colorful it will have you drooling for the real thing in no time. Or better yet, paint up a set so you can serve dessert at your Halloween gathering.

Supplies

glass plate

PermEnamel Surface Conditioner

PermEnamel Clear Gloss Glaze

black graphite paper

stylus

Brushes

large glaze brush

no. 8 flat

$\frac{1}{2}$-inch (13mm) angle

no. 1 liner

Delta Air Dry PermEnamels

Ultra White	Citrus Yellow	Tangerine	Harvest Orange	Ultra Black

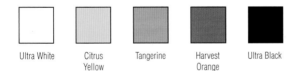

Tip ●

In order for this plate to be used with dry or wet foods, you will paint with a technique called reverse painting. So nothing will come directly in contact with the paint, you'll paint the underside of the plate. Everything has to be done backwards. You'll paint the highlights first, then shade and finally basecoat. If you stay within your pattern lines, you can erase them before you glaze.

Enlarge or reduce this pattern to fit your project.

1 Prepare the Plate

Turn your plate upside down and clean the underside of the plate with surface conditioner and a paper towel. Let dry. Be careful not to put your fingers on the area where the design will be. Transfer the pattern using black graphite paper and a stylus. If you have trouble seeing the transfer, make sure the surface is dry and try a newer piece of graphite paper.

2 Basecoat and Highlight

Using a no. 8 flat brush and Ultra White, basecoat all the candy corn tips. This should be about one-third of the area you have for each candy corn. This will take at least two coats, but if it's still transparent after two, give it a third. It's very important that you let each coat dry completely so you don't lift the paint. If you paint more than one plate, there will be plenty of time for drying. When you finish the last one, you are ready to go back to the first plate again. With your liner brush and Ultra White, place a highlight line along the top edge of the other two sections. We placed this along the side closest to the center of the plate.

3 Shade the Candy Corn

Using a ½-inch (13mm) angle brush and Harvest Orange, float along the outer edge of the other two sections opposite the highlight.

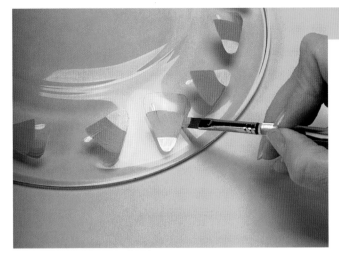

4 Basecoat the Middle Section

Basecoat the middle section with your no. 8 flat and Tangerine. This will take two coats and cover another third of your area.

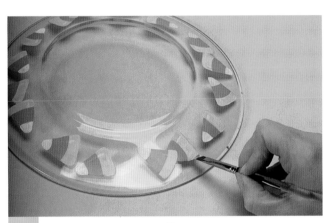

5 Basecoat the End Section

Still using a no. 8 flat, basecoat the ends with two coats of Citrus Yellow.

6 Glaze

Using the no. 1 liner and Ultra Black, make a squiggly line to frame the center of the plate. Using a large soft brush, glaze the plate with the PermEnamel Clear Gloss Glaze. We only glazed over the painted area. Follow the manufacturer's directions.

These plates can be hand washed and withstand heat of 350°F (318°C). We do not recommend putting them in the dishwasher, which may go above this temperature.

Bat
Placemat

Paint a set of these for the family and your little ones will rush to the table at mealtime. With these placemats the excitement of Halloween will never be hard to find. I can hear it now, "I'm going to be a scarecrow and you can be a princess." What a fun time!

Supplies

oval, primed canvas placemat

black and white graphite paper

stylus

Brushes

$\frac{1}{2}$-inch (13mm) angle

$\frac{5}{8}$-inch (16mm) angle

no. 10 flat

$\frac{3}{4}$-inch (19mm) flat

no. 1 liner

no. 4 fabric scrubber

no. 6 sable

Delta Ceramcoat Acrylic Paints

| Opaque Yellow | Purple Smoke | Black | Oyster White | Tangerine | Turquoise |

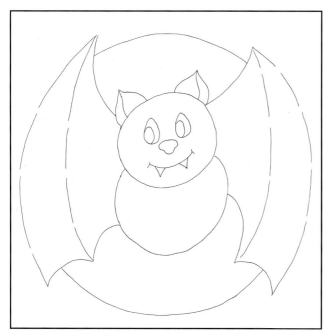

Enlarge or reduce the pattern to fit your project.

1 Basecoat

Transfer the pattern, excluding the details, using black graphite paper and a stylus. Using a ³/₄-inch (19mm) flat brush, basecoat the moon in Opaque Yellow, the bat in Purple Smoke, and the negative space behind the moon and inside the bat ears in Black. Let dry. Apply the pattern for the eyes and teeth using white graphite paper. Basecoat the eyes and teeth in Oyster White and let dry. Reapply your pattern detail, again using the white graphite paper and stylus.

2 Shade the Moon

Load your no. 6 sable brush with Tangerine. Pounce color along the outer edges of the moon, using a heavier touch toward the outer edge and a softer touch as you move to the center.

3 Sharpen the Edges

Sharpen the edges and fill in the holes by floating Tangerine with your ⁵/₈-inch (16mm) angle brush along the outer edge.

4 Shade the Bat

Using your ⅝-inch (16mm) angle and Black, float along the outer edge of the bat's body, ears, wings, and all around the head. Float on the ribs of the bat wings.

5 Highlight Your Bat

Using the no. 4 fabric scrubber brush and Turquoise, scrub color in each of the bat's wing sections, body, head and ears. Keep this color out of your shaded areas. Clean your brush, and scrub on the cheeks with Tangerine.

6 Add the Finishing Touches

With a no. 10 flat and Black, basecoat the pupil of the bat's eyes and nose. Use a no. 1 liner brush and Black thinned with water to outline the entire eye. Outline the teeth and place your smile line.

Using the liner and thinned Turquoise, outline the ribs of the wings. Paint an Oyster White comma stroke across the top of the nose. Use the end of the brush handle to dot on an Oyster White highlight on each cheek and two in the lower right side of each eye.

Varnish both sides of the placemat with at least two coats of your favorite water-based varnish.

Ghostly Invitation

F all is in the air. The leaves are turning colors, the wind has a slight chill, and thoughts of Halloween begin to stir. It's party time! After the guest list has been written, a handmade invitation is in order. This ghostly one is perfect to let all your friends know that the fun is about to begin.

Supplies

4³/4" × 7" (12cm × 18cm) blank greeting card with envelope

8" × 12" (20cm × 31cm) sheet of vellum

black graphite paper

stylus

tacky glue

Brushes

no. 0 liner

¹/2-inch (13mm) flat

Delta Ceramcoat Acrylic Paint

Tangerine   White   Black   Nightfall Blue   Quaker Grey

Enlarge or reduce this pattern to fit your project. For this surface it appears at full size.

1 Transfer the Pattern and Basecoat

Using a stylus and black graphite paper, transfer the oval pattern. Basecoat the entire oval using a ½-inch (13mm) flat brush and Tangerine. Apply the rest of the pattern. Basecoat the ghost with several layers of White. Using the no. 0 liner brush and Black, basecoat the bats. Using Nightfall Blue and the ½-inch (13mm) flat, float a shade down the left side of the large ghost. Next, shade the left side of the right arm, along the edge of the oval where the left ghost is, and on the left side of the right arm.

2   Paint the Features and Details

Using a no. 0 liner and Black, add features to the faces and outline the oval. Using Quaker Grey and a very narrow float, highlight the top of the bat's wings. With a no. 0 liner and Quaker Grey, add lines to the bat wings.

You're Invited

What:

When:

Where:

3   Add the Text

Handwrite the text on the vellum or use a creepy computer font like we did. Glue the vellum inside the invitation.

Fill in the information for your party and have a wonderful time!

Haunted House Invitation

This ghostly haunted house offers another option for a great invitation.

First, basecoat the entire card, front and back, with Purple Smoke and the $^3/4$-inch (19mm) flat. With the $^1/2$-inch (13mm) flat, basecoat the house and tree with Black and the windows with Opaque Yellow. Shade the left side of the windows with Burnt Sienna on the $^1/2$-inch (13mm) flat. With Quaker Grey on the $^1/2$-inch (13mm) flat, float in the shutters and the door. Use the no. 6 filbert to basecoat the ghost with White and add facial features with Black and the no. 1 liner. Add a float of Nightfall Blue with the $^1/2$-inch (13mm) flat down the left side of the ghost.

Supplies
$4^3/4$" × 7" (12cm × 18cm) blank greeting card with envelope

white graphite paper

stylus

Brushes
no. 1 liner

no. 6 filbert

$^3/4$-inch (19mm) flat

$^1/2$-inch (13mm) flat

Delta Ceramcoat Acrylic Paints
Black

Burnt Sienna

Nightfall Blue

Opaque Yellow

Purple Smoke

Quaker Grey

White

The Eyes Have It Invitation

Supplies

4 ¾" × 7" (12cm × 18cm) blank greeting card with envelope

white graphite paper

stylus

sea sponge

Brushes

no. 1 liner

no. 6 filbert

¾-inch (19mm) flat

½-inch (13mm) flat

stippler or old worn brush

Delta Ceramcoat Acrylic Paints

Black

Midnight Blue

Poppy Orange

Pumpkin

Quaker Grey

Seminole Green

White

All eyes are watching you. At least it appears that way with this invitation. Who knows what lurks behind those shadows!

Basecoat the front of the card with Midnight Blue and your ¾-inch flat brush. Basecoat the moon with Pumpkin and your no. 6 filbert. Let dry and sponge some Poppy Orange over it. With your scruffy brush and Midnight Blue, plus White, stipple in the tree. Use your ½-inch (13mm) flat to lighten areas of the tree with Quaker Grey. Basecoat the holes in the tree with Black and a no. 6 filbert. Add eyes in the holes with White and a no. 1 liner brush, and then add a Black dot to each. Base in the tombstone with Quaker Grey and a no. 6 filbert. Add the writing to the tombstone with Black and a no. 1 liner brush. With a no. 6 filbert, basecoat the pumpkin with Poppy Orange, then add leaves with Seminole Green.

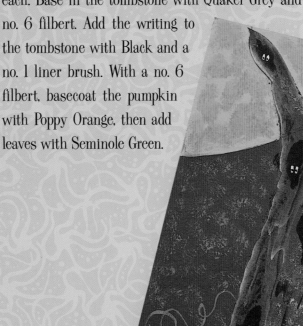

Pumpkin Saucer

This piece is not only really cute, but also very economical. We used an ordinary clay saucer. The size of the saucer would determine how you use it. Wouldn't it be cute filled with candy for your favorite goblins? Or start with a larger size and use it for chips at your Halloween bash. It's sure to be a smash!

Supplies

clay saucer
sea sponge
black graphite paper
stylus
water-based varnish

Brushes

no. 1 liner
no. 6 filbert
$1/2$-inch (13mm) angle
no. 8 flat
$3/4$-inch (19mm) glaze brush

Delta Ceramcoat Acrylic Paint

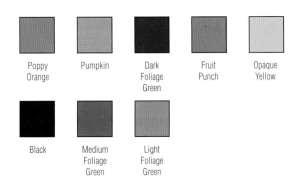

Poppy Orange	Pumpkin	Dark Foliage Green	Fruit Punch	Opaque Yellow

Black	Medium Foliage Green	Light Foliage Green

Enlarge or reduce this pattern to fit your project. For this surface it appears at full size.

1 Start Sponging the Background

With a dampened sea sponge, sponge Poppy Orange on the inside and top rim of the saucer.

2 Finish the Background

Using the uncleaned sponge, pick up some Pumpkin and sponge over the first color, letting some of the first show through. The area should now be completely covered.

3 Basecoat Under the Saucer

Basecoat the underside of the saucer with Dark Foliage Green using a ³/₄-inch (19mm) glaze brush.

4 Float the Sections

Apply the pattern using white graphite paper and your stylus. Using a ¹/₂-inch (13mm) angle brush and Fruit Punch, float to the right of the right section and to the left of both the left and center sections.

5 | Basecoat the Pumpkin Face

Basecoat the cut edge of the pumpkin's eyes, nose and mouth with a no. 8 flat brush and Opaque Yellow. Basecoat the rest of the eyes, nose and mouth with Black. Basecoat the leaves with Medium Foliage Green.

6 | Shade the Pumpkin

Using your ½-inch (13mm) angle brush and Poppy Orange, float across both ends of the cut edge of each eye section. Next, float across the bend in the center of this same section. Then float the nose cut on each end. Finally, float the mouth cut at each outer end, and in the two center bends. Float across the bottom of the leaves with Dark Foliage Green.

8 | Add Stems

Using a no. 1 liner brush and thinned Dark Foliage Green, add your stems and a few curlicues. With Black on your liner, outline the eyes, nose and mouth.

7 | Highlight the Foliage

Float a highlight across the top of the leaves with Light Foliage Green using your ½-inch (13mm) angle brush.

9 | Add Filler Leaves

Use a no. 6 filbert brush and Dark Foliage Green to place a few one-stroke leaves for filler and to soften the face.

Varnish with two to three coats of your favorite water-based varnish.

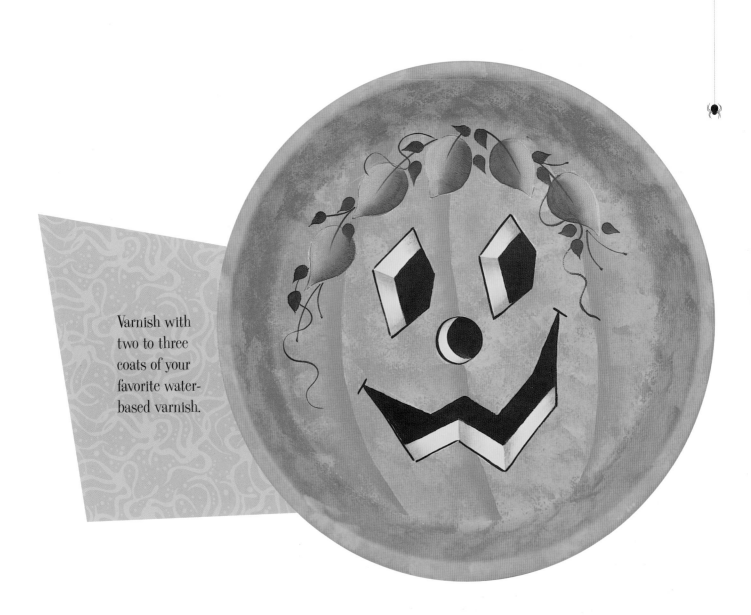

Halloween Welcome Sign

W hether you are six or sixty, this neat sign will give all a warm welcome. Its many faces of Halloween will bring a smile to visitors and let them know the season is approaching. Hanging either inside or outside, you're sure to get happy responses.

Supplies

7" × 24" (18cm × 61cm) sign board

sawtooth hanger

Fruitwood Gel Stain

black and white graphite paper

stylus

water-based varnish

Brushes

no. 1 liner

no. 4 filbert

no. 8 flat

1/2-inch (13mm) flat

1/2-inch (13mm) comb

old worn brush

2-inch (51mm) sponge brush

Delta Ceramcoat Acrylic Paint

| Black | Midnight Blue | Light Ivory | White | Mello Yellow | Crocus Yellow | Charcoal |

| Drizzle Grey | Medium Flesh | Lime Green | Burnt Sienna | Poppy Orange | Red Iron Oxide | Seminole Green |

| Dark Forest Green | Apple Green | Opaque Yellow | Dark Burnt Umber |

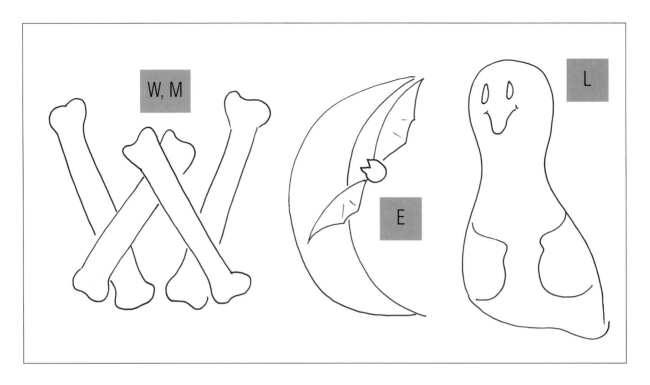

Enlarge or reduce these patterns to fit your project.

1 Prepare Surface and Transfer Pattern

Sand the surface and wipe clean. Using the 2-inch (51mm) sponge brush, stain the entire board with the Fruitwood Gel Stain. With the sponge brush and Black, paint the frame of the board. Transfer the pattern lines with black graphite paper and your stylus. Use white graphite for the pattern on the frame.

2 Basecoat the Letters

Using the ½-inch (13mm) flat, or the brush that is most comfortable for you, basecoat the letters as follows:

W, M, and L—basecoat: Light Ivory
E—basecoat: Mello Yellow
E—bat: Charcoal
C—hat and clothing: Charcoal
C—face and neck: Medium Flesh
C—hair: Drizzle Grey
C—hatband: Poppy Orange
O—jack-o-lantern: Poppy Orange
O—leaves: Seminole Green

3 Shade and Highlight the W. M. and L

Using your ½-inch (13mm) flat brush and Midnight Blue, float a watery shade down the left side of each bone. Float a shade on the bottom bone at the overlap. Highlight the right side of each bone with White. Using Nightfall Blue and your ½-inch (13mm) flat, float a watery shade along ghost's left side and around the arms. Float a highlight with White down the right side of the ghost and around the arms. Using your no. 1 liner brush and Black, basecoat the eyes and mouth. Add a White highlight in each eye at 2 o'clock with the handle-tip end of your liner.

4 Shade and Highlight the E

Float a shade down the left side of the moon with your ½-inch (13mm) flat and Crocus Yellow. Float a highlight down the right side of the moon with White. Shade the underside of the wings and body of the bat with your no. 8 flat brush and Black. Highlight the top of the wings and body of the bat with a very narrow float of Drizzle Grey. Using a no. 1 liner, add two small dots for eyes and two thin lines to the wings with Drizzle Grey.

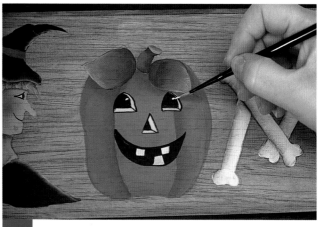

5 Shade and Highlight the C

Make a wash with Lime Green and go all over the skin area using a ½-inch (13mm) flat. Add a few warts of Lime Green. Continue to use your flat to float Burnt Sienna under the chin, along the top of the clothing, and along the hairline. With your no. 1 liner and Black, put in the eye and the mouth. Switch to your ½-inch (13mm) comb brush. Add lines to the hair with White, then more lines with Lime Green, and then more lines with Black. Using your old worn brush, scrub the cheeks with Poppy Orange. With Red Iron Oxide and your ½-inch (13mm) flat, float a shade on each side of the hatband. Float a shade down the left side of the hat and across the hatband top with Black and your ½-inch (13mm) flat. Continue to use the flat and float a shade on the hair directly under the hat with Black.

6 Shade and Highlight the O

Using a ½-inch (13mm) flat and Red Iron Oxide, float down the front of the jack-o-lantern's face to define the sections. With Dark Forest Green, shade the stem end of each leaf and the underside of the stem. Continue to use your flat and float a highlight on each leaf with Apple Green at the lower part of the left leaf and the upper part of the right leaf. Highlight the topside of the stem with Apple Green. With your no. 8 flat, basecoat the cut section of the eyes and nose with Opaque Yellow. Clean the brush and basecoat the remainder of the eyes, nose and mouth with Black. With Light Ivory, basecoat the teeth using your no. 8 flat. Using Black and your no. 1 liner, outline the eyes and nose. Clean the brush and add a highlight to each eye at 2 o'clock with White.

7 Finish the Letters

With Black and a no. 1 liner, outline each letter.

8 Basecoat the Spider and Candy Corn

Using a no. 1 liner and Black, basecoat the spider web and the spider. Using a no. 4 filbert brush and White, basecoat the candy corn.

9 Finish the Candy Corn

With your no. 4 filbert and Opaque Yellow, add a top stripe to each kernel of corn. Clean the brush and use Poppy Orange to add a stripe in the middle of each kernel. With your no. 8 flat, shade the bottom of each kernel with Red Iron Oxide. Add a highlight to each kernel with your no. 1 liner and White.

With your ½-inch (13mm) flat and Dark Burnt Umber, add a shadow down the left side of each letter. When dry, varnish with three to four coats of a water-based varnish with your sponge brush. Add a sawtooth hanger to the back.

Spider Basket

T his would be a great project for you and your special little goblins to do together. They would have a great time sponging the colors on the sides. Not only is it cute on the basket, it'd be great on a canvas bag for your goblins' trick or treats.

Delta Ceramcoat Acrylic Paints

| Purple Smoke | Black | Tangerine | Turquoise | Oyster White |

Supplies
round, wooden basket
sea sponge
white graphite paper
stylus
water-based varnish

Brushes
no. 1 liner
no. 4 fabric scrubber
$1/2$-inch (13mm) angle
no. 6 flat
$3/4$-inch (19mm) glaze brush

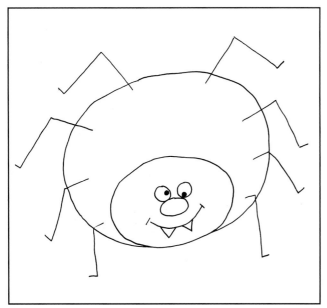

Enlarge or reduce this pattern to fit your project.

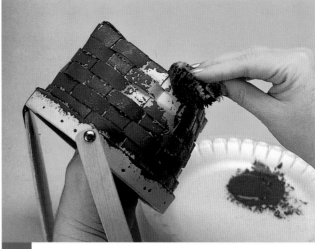

1 Sponge First Color

With a dampened sea sponge, pick up Purple Smoke. Sponge this around the outside and bottom of your basket. It will be easier if you use lots of paint on your sponge so it can ooze into the little cracks and crevices.

2 Sponge Second Color

While this is still wet, pick up some Black and sponge this all around. This will give you a nice two-tone effect.

3 Basecoat Lid, Rim and Handle

Using your ¾-inch (19mm) brush, basecoat the lid in Purple Smoke. We did the side edges and the underside of the lid too. Use Tangerine on the rim and handle.

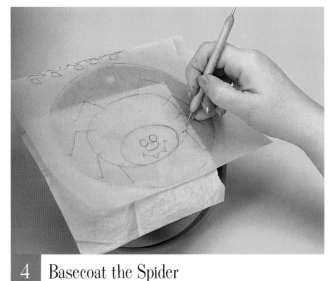

4 Basecoat the Spider

Apply your pattern for the spider using your white graphite paper and stylus. Basecoat the spider's body and head with Black using your ³/₄-inch (19mm) glaze brush.

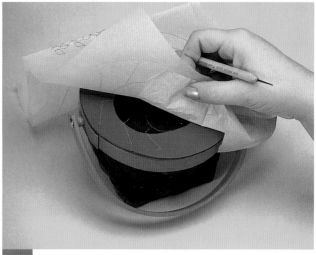

5 Transfer the Detail

Reapply the detail to the spider with the white graphite paper and stylus.

6 Shade the Spider

With your ½-inch (13mm) angle and Turquoise, float around the outside edge of the body and head. Paint the nose in solid using your no. 6 flat brush.

7 Detail the Face

Using Oyster White and a no. 6 flat, paint in the eyes and teeth. Scrub in the cheeks with Tangerine using a no. 4 fabric scrubber. Now with the no. 1 liner and Oyster White, paint in a comma stroke along the top of the nose and a smile line above the teeth.

8 Finish the Lid

Using your no. 1 liner and thinned Black, paint in the spider's legs. Give the spider fur by painting short, erratic lines all around the outer edges of the head and body. With the handle end of your brush, place a pupil dot in each eye. To make him look a little loopy, I placed the left eye dot at 3 o'clock and the right one at 6 o'clock. Now use your no. 1 liner and thinned Tangerine to paint a wavy line around the outer edge of the lid.

9 Add Rim Details

Using your no. 1 liner and thinned Black, paint the spokes on each of the cobwebs. Then go back and paint the connecting lines, forming each web.

10 Add Finishing Touches

Using the large end of your stylus and Turquoise, place a dot between each web on the rim.

Varnish with your favorite water-based varnish.

Pumpkin Basket

This piece would make a really cute companion piece for the Pumpkin Saucer. For this piece, you will be using the same techniques that you used for the saucer.

For the sides of the basket use a dampened sea sponge to sponge on Poppy Orange and then Pumpkin (see page 48). Use a 3/4-inch (19mm) glaze brush to basecoat the lid of the basket in Poppy Orange. Paint the rim and handle with Dark Foliage Green using a no. 8 flat. Apply the Pumpkin Saucer pattern, sized to fit, and paint the lid following the directions for the saucer. Paint the vine on the rim by adding Black to Dark Foliage Green and painting a loose vine all around the edge using a no. 1 liner. Next, using a no. 6 filbert brush and Medium Foliage Green, paint one-stroke leaves around the vine. Repeat this, making some more leaves in Light Foliage Green. Paint curlicues with Light Foliage Green and varnish.

Supplies
round, wooden basket
sea sponge
white graphite paper
stylus
water-based varnish

Brushes
no. 1 liner
no. 6 filbert
1/2-inch (13mm) angle
no. 8 flat
3/4-inch (19mm) glaze

Delta Ceramcoat Acrylic Paints
Opaque Yellow
Light Foliage Green
Pumpkin
Dark Foliage Green
Black
Medium Foliage Green
Poppy Orange
Fruit Punch

Boo Mailbox Cover

T his festive mailbox cover is a great way to show you're in the spirit of Halloween. Simply adhere it to the side of your mailbox and get ready for all the nice remarks to come your way. No mailbox? It also works great on metal doors.

Supplies

12" × 18" (31cm × 45cm) piece of magnetic sheeting

black and white graphite paper

stylus

exterior varnish

sharp scissors

Brushes

no. 1 liner

no. 8 flat

1/2-inch (13mm) flat

3/4-inch (19mm) flat

old worn brush

Delta Ceramcoat Acrylic Paint

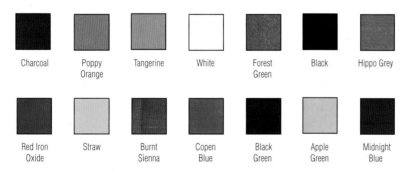

| Charcoal | Poppy Orange | Tangerine | White | Forest Green | Black | Hippo Grey |

| Red Iron Oxide | Straw | Burnt Sienna | Copen Blue | Black Green | Apple Green | Midnight Blue |

Enlarge or reduce this pattern to fit your project.

1 Transfer the Pattern and Basecoat

Transfer the pattern to the magnetic sheeting using black graphite and a stylus. Using your ³/₄-inch (19mm) brush, basecoat the hat with Charcoal, the middle pumpkin with Poppy Orange, and the pumpkin on the right and the hatband with Tangerine. With White and a ¹/₂-inch (13mm) flat brush, basecoat the BOO. Using Forest Green and a no. 8 flat, basecoat the stems of the pumpkins.

2 Shade the Hat

With Black on your ¹/₂-inch (13mm) flat, float a shade down the sides of the hat, above the hatband, and on the brim where it goes behind the main section of the hat. With an old worn brush, scrub a highlight down the center of the hat and across the front brim with Hippo Grey. With Red Iron Oxide and your ¹/₂-inch (13mm) flat, shade both sides of the hatband. Place a back-to-back float down the center of the hatband with Straw. (This may take several coats to achieve a bright look.)

3 Shade the Pumpkins

Using white graphite paper, transfer the facial features to the middle pumpkin. Using Red Iron Oxide and a ¹/₂-inch (13mm) flat, shade the middle pumpkin. Float down the sections, under the stem, and on the pumpkin where it's behind the hat. Using Poppy Orange, shade the pumpkin on the right. Float down the sections and under the stem using your ¹/₂-inch (13mm) flat.

4 Deepen the Shading

With Burnt Sienna and your ¹/₂-inch (13mm) flat, deepen the shading on the pumpkin on the right. This second shading should be smaller and not cover all of the previous shading.

5 Base in the Facial Features

With your no. 1 liner brush and Black, basecoat the eyes, nose and mouth.

6 Add Facial Details

Using a no. 1 liner and White, highlight the eyes at 2 o'clock and put in the teeth. With Copen Blue and your ¹/₂-inch (13mm) flat, float the irises in the eyes.

7 Shade and Highlight the Stems

Shade the left side, under the "cut" section and the bottom of each stem with Black Green and your ½-inch (13mm) flat. Add detail lines on the stems with a no. 1 liner and Black Green. With Apple Green and a ½-inch (13mm) flat, float a highlight next to the Black Green float that goes across the "cut" section of the stem. Using Straw and a ½-inch (13mm) flat, gently tap in the highlights on the top of each section of both pumpkins.

8 Shade the BOO

With Midnight Blue and your ½-inch (13mm) flat, float a shade on the left side of the BOO letters. Protect the design with several layers of exterior varnish.

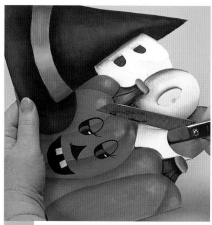

9 Cut Out the Design

Using sharp scissors, cut out the design. You may need a smaller pair of scissors to cut out the insides of the Os.

Place the magnet on your mailbox and enjoy!

Refrigerator Magnets

U se leftover parts of the magnetic sheeting to make these fun and festive refrigerator magnets. Any of the designs in this book would make a terrific magnet—just reduce the designs to the size that you want and follow the painting instructions.

Witch's Hat Magnet

Reduce the hat pattern from this project or draw your own hat and transfer the pattern to the sheeting. Using your 1/2-inch (13mm) flat, basecoat the entire hat with Charcoal. Float down both sides and across the top of the brim with Black and your 1/2-inch (13mm) flat. Using the no. 4 flat, basecoat the hatband with Pumpkin. Float a shade on each side of the band with Red Iron Oxide and your no. 4 flat. Place a back-to-back float in the center of the hatband with a 2:1 mix of Pumpkin and White with your no. 4 flat. Spray with varnish.

Candy Corn Magnet

Use the candy corn pattern from the Candy Corn Dish or draw your own, then transfer the pattern to the sheeting. Basecoat the top section of the kernel with Opaque Yellow, the middle section with Poppy Orange and the bottom section with White using your no. 4 flat. With Black and your no. 1 liner outline the kernel. Spray with interior satin varnish.

Supplies
magnetic sheeting
black graphite paper
spray varnish

Brushes
no. 1 liner
no. 4 flat
1/2-inch (13mm) flat

Delta Ceramcoat Acrylic Paints
Charcoal
Black
Pumpkin
Red Iron Oxide
White
Opaque Yellow
Poppy Orange

Creepy Cauldron

R emember all those creepy movies we loved as kids? At Halloween our parents would play our favorite scary movie. We loved Frankenstein and Dracula—the more ghosts and skeletons the better. We have tried to capture all that fun in this cauldron. I use this for my Halloween candy, so when trick-or-treaters visit my castle they get a little spooking.

Supplies

black plastic cauldron
white and black graphite paper
stylus
spray varnish

Brushes

no. 1 liner
no. 3 round
no. 4 fabric scrubber
3/8-inch (9mm) angle
1/2-inch (13mm) angle
no. 6 flat
no. 8 flat
no. 12 flat

Delta Ceramcoat Acrylic Paints

| Black | Eucalyptus | Kelly Green | Oyster White | Poppy Orange | Purple Smoke | Turquoise |

Quaker Grey

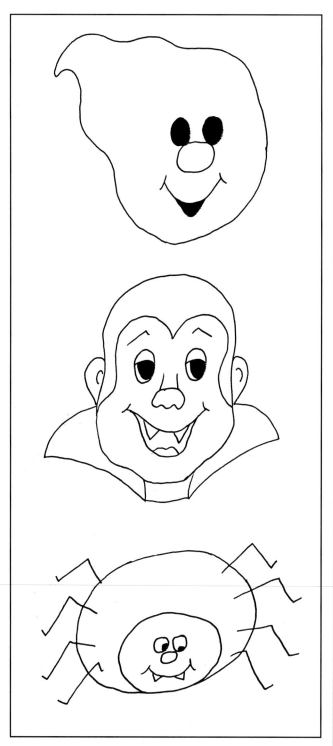

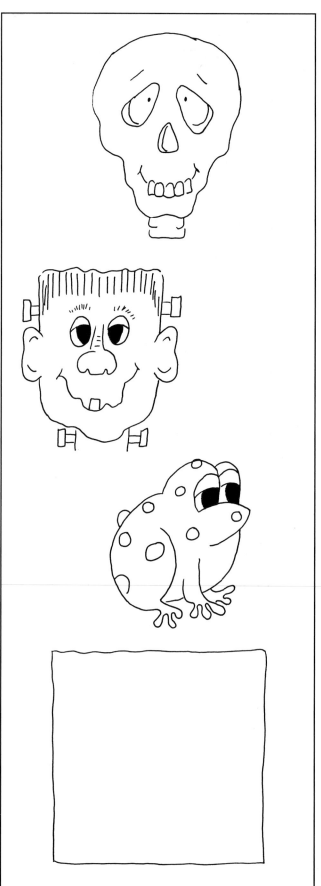

Enlarge or reduce these patterns to fit your project.

1 Prepare the Surface & Basecoat

Spray the outside of your cauldron with the varnish. This allows the paint to grab onto something. Apply your pattern for each square with white graphite paper and your stylus. Basecoat each square with a couple of coats of Purple Smoke. When this is dry, use your no. 1 liner and thinned Poppy Orange to paint a curvy line around each square.

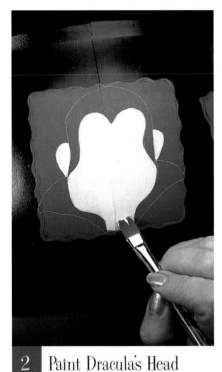

2 Paint Dracula's Head

Transfer the patterns onto the squares with white graphite paper and a stylus. With your no. 12 flat brush, basecoat the count's head, ears and neck in Oyster White.

3 Basecoat Face

Apply the face details with black graphite paper and a stylus. With a no. 8 flat brush and Black, basecoat his hair, cape, eyes and the inside of his mouth. Use Poppy Orange to basecoat the tongue.

4 Shade Dracula

With Eucalyptus and a ½-inch (13mm) angle, shade the top of the count's face, below the hairline. Float around the mouth, along the top of the nose, inside the ears, under the chin and across both eyelids. Scrub in the cheeks with the no. 4 fabric scrubber brush and Poppy Orange.

5 Highlight Dracula

With a ½-inch (13mm) angle and Turquoise, highlight the top of the head and along the top of the cape.

7 Add Eye Sparkle

With Oyster White and your no. 1 liner, place two dots in the lower left sides of the eyes. Place a larger dot in the upper right side.

6 Add Detail to Dracula

With a no. 1 liner and thinned Black, detail the eyes and around the nose and mouth. Line the inside of the ears, across the chin and the bottom of the neck. Give him eyebrows.

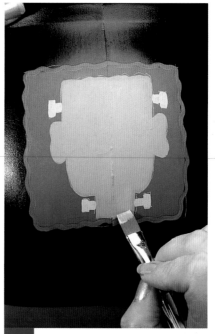

8 Basecoat Frank

Basecoat Frank's head with Eucalyptus, using your no. 12 flat. Add the screws with Quaker Grey. Apply the pattern for the face detail using white graphite paper and your stylus.

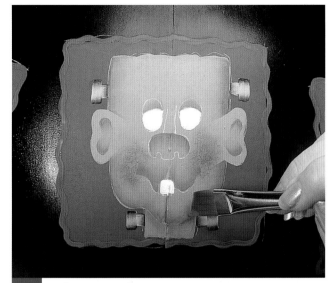

9 Shade Frank

Paint the lower part of each eye and his tooth in Oyster White, using the no. 8 flat. Scrub in his cheeks with the no. 4 fabric scrubber and Poppy Orange. Use your ½-inch (13mm) angle to shade with Kelly Green. Float across the eyelid, across the top of the nose, inside the ears, under the chin, around the outside of the face, and above the mouth line. Shade the bolts with Black and the ⅜-inch (9mm) angle brush. Float next to the head and along the outer edge of the bolts.

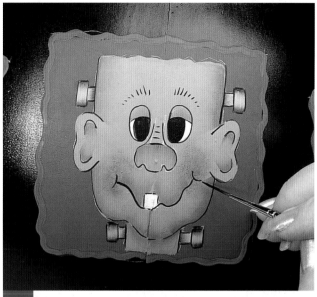

10 Add Face Detail

Paint the pupil with Black using a no. 6 flat. Thin the Black and use your no. 1 liner to add eyebrows and outline Frank's head, eyes, nose, mouth and tooth. Loosely outline the bolts.

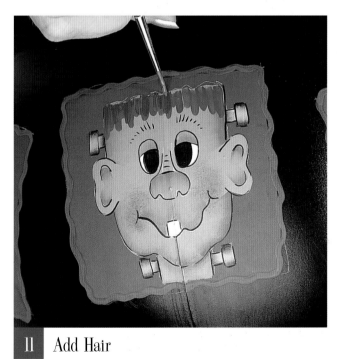

11 Add Hair

With a no. 3 round, stroke in the hair, first in Kelly Green, and then again in Poppy Orange.

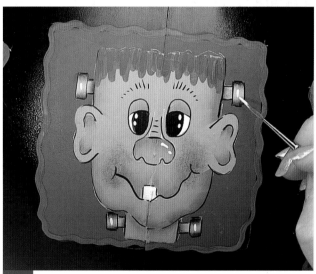

12 Add Finishing Details

Using a no. 1 liner and White, place two highlight dots in the outer edge of each eye. Place a comma stroke across the top of the nose. Highlight the bolts as well.

13   Paint the Frog

- Using a no. 8 flat, basecoat the frog belly and lower part of the eyes in Oyster White, the body in Eucalyptus, the warts in Turquoise, and the tongue in Poppy Orange.
- Shade with Kelly Green and your ½-inch (13mm) angle. Float across the back, down to the toes on the back leg, down the left side of the front legs, across the top of the mouth, along the inside edges of the underbelly, across the eyelids, and on the left side of each wart.
- Scrub a highlight of Oyster White through the center of the unshaded areas using a no. 4 fabric scrubber. Basecoat the pupils of the eyes with a no. 6 flat and Black, and add highlight dots of Oyster White to the eyes. Outline the frog with Black on the no. 1 liner.

14   Paint the Skeleton

- With a no. 12 flat, basecoat the skeleton in Oyster White. Apply the pattern using black graphite paper and a stylus.
- Basecoat the eyes and nose with Black and a no. 6 flat.
- Float a shade of Eucalyptus around the outside edge of the head, under the chin and the neck vertebra, using a ½-inch (13mm) angle.
- Using the ⅜-inch (19mm) angle, float Turquoise C-strokes in the lower part of the eyes, then float a line just inside the left side of the nose.
- With your no. 1 liner and thinned Black, give him eyebrows; outline the whole head, neck and vertebra; and outline his teeth and mouth. With the handle of your brush, put a dot in each eye with Oyster White.

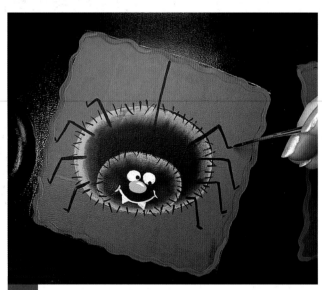

15   Paint the Spider

Follow the directions for the Spider Basket on page 49.

16 | Paint the Ghost

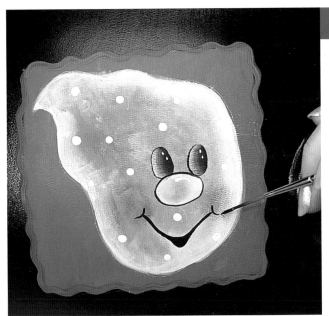

• With your no. 12 flat brush, basecoat the ghost with thinned Oyster White. When this dries, float around the outside edge of the ghost's head with the same color. Then float around the outside edge of each eye, around the inside of the nose, and around the mouth.

• Scrub in the cheeks with the no. 4 fabric scrubber brush and Poppy Orange.

• Basecoat the eyes and mouth with Black. Then outline the mouth, nose and eyes with your no. 1 liner and thinned Black.

• Float a C-stroke of Oyster White along the left side of each eye, just inside the edge. With your no. 1 liner and Oyster White, put two dots in the upper right corner of each eye. Add a comma stroke along the top of the nose. With the handle end of a brush, place Oyster white dots over the head.

Finish by giving the cauldron a couple of good coats of spray varnish.

Spooky Wreath

Nothing says welcome more than a great looking wreath. This one is such fun to make! Whether you hang it indoors or on the front door, you will enjoy the atmosphere it provides.

Delta Ceramcoat Acrylic Paint

 Black

 Apple Green

 Adobe Red

 White

 Opaque Yellow

 Quaker Grey

 Tangerine

 Dark Forest Green

 Seminole Green

Supplies

14" (36cm) grapevine wreath

fall-colored leaves

$2/3$ yard (60cm) of $1/2$" (1cm) white satin ribbon

$1 1/3$ yards (122cm) of $1/2$" (1cm) orange satin ribbon

2 yards (183cm) of $1/2$" (1cm) black satin ribbon

large Halloween bow

6 primed canvas coasters

hole puncher

plastic spider

tacky glue

black and white graphite paper

stylus

Brushes

no. 0 liner

no. 1 liner

no. 4 flat

$1/2$-inch (13mm) flat

$3/4$-inch (19mm) flat

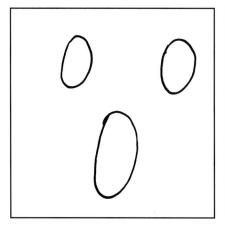

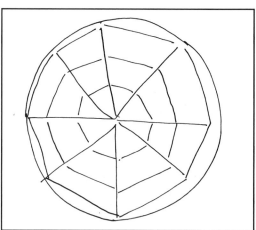

Enlarge or reduce these patterns to fit your project.

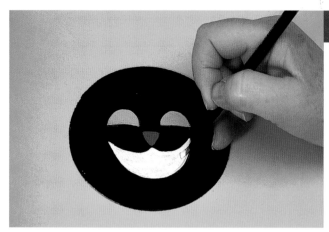

1 Basecoat the Cat

Basecoat the entire coaster with Black and a ¾-inch (19mm) flat brush. Transfer the cat pattern with white graphite paper and a stylus. Using a no. 4 flat brush, basecoat the eyes with Apple Green, the nose with Adobe Red, and the mouth with White.

2 Add Details to the Features

With Black and a no. 1 liner brush, add pupils to the eyes and paint the lines between the teeth. Switch to your no. 0 liner brush and use White to add the whiskers and eyelashes. Then add the lines between the eyes, the eye highlights, and the shine line on the top of the nose. Float on the ears with White and your ½-inch (13mm) flat brush.

3 Basecoat the Witch

Basecoat the entire coaster with Opaque Yellow and your ¾-inch (19mm) flat. Transfer the witch pattern. Using your no. 4 flat brush, basecoat the witch with Black. With black graphite paper and a stylus, add the stars. First dip the large end of the stylus into White.

4 Finish the Stars

Then touch down on the surface and pull the points of the stars from the center.

5 Paint the Ghost, Spider and Jack-o-Lanterns

• To make the ghost, basecoat the entire coaster with White and the ¾-inch (19mm) flat. Transfer the design with black graphite paper and a stylus. Paint the facial features with Black and a no. 1 liner.

• To make the spider web ornament, basecoat the entire coaster with Black. Transfer the pattern with white graphite paper or freehand it. Using a no. 1 liner and Quaker Grey, line the web. Glue on the plastic spider.

• For the two jack-o-lanterns, basecoat the entire coasters with Tangerine. Transfer the patterns with black graphite paper.

• To paint the scowling jack-o-lantern, basecoat the eyes with Black and a no. 1 liner, and the nose and mouth with Adobe Red. Outline the eyes with Opaque Yellow. Clean the brush and outline the nose, and add the eyebrows and the lip line with Black. Tap a White highlight in each eye at 2 o'clock.

• To paint the leafy jack-o-lantern basecoat the mouth, eyes and nose with Black and a no. 1 liner. Clean the brush and use Opaque Yellow to outline the eyes, nose and mouth. Add the teeth with White and place a highlight in each eye at 2 o'clock. Stroke in the leaves with both Dark Forest Green and Seminole Green blended on a no. 4 filbert. Add vein lines and tendrils to the leaves with a no. 1 liner and Dark Forest Green.

6 Prepare for Hanging

With your hole puncher, place two holes about an inch apart (2.5cm) at the top of each ornament. Thread ribbons through the holes.

Run the ribbons through the grapevine wreath to attach the ornaments. With tacky glue, attach the leaves to the grapevine. Add the bow for the final touch.

Halloween Tree Ornaments

A Halloween tree is so much fun. It could decorate an entryway or a special place in a room. Place some orange lights, a few fall colored leaves, and these great ornaments on the tree, and you will have an accent piece to sparkle any place. These ornaments are painted with the same colors and directions as the ones on the Spooky Wreath with the addition of a Moon and Stars ornament.

To paint the Moon and Stars Ornament, basecoat the entire ornament with Midnight Blue and a ¾-inch (19mm) flat. Transfer the pattern with white graphite paper and a stylus. Basecoat the moon with Crocus Yellow using a no. 6 filbert. Using White and your stylus, add the stars. To finish, spray with interior varnish.

Supplies

2½" (6cm) satin painted glass ornaments
white graphite paper
stylus
interior varnish

Brushes

no. 6 filbert
¾-inch (19mm) flat

Delta Ceramcoat Acrylic Paints

Crocus Yellow
Midnight Blue
White

Refer to step 5 of this project for painting this jack-o-lantern.

Refer to steps 3 and 4 of this project for painting this witch and stars.

Refer to steps 1 and 2 of this project for painting this cat.

Scarecrow Yard Sign

I don't know if this scarecrow will chase any crows away! He looks too friendly to me. But place him by the front entrance and he's sure to bring a smile as he greets all your guests.

Supplies

$^1/_2$" (1cm) plywood

wood sealer

wooden stake

wood glue

medium- to fine-grade sandpaper

black and white graphite paper

stylus

sea sponge

water-based varnish

Brushes

no. 1 liner

no. 8 fabric scrubber

$^5/_8$-inch (16mm) angle

no. 8 flat

$^3/_4$-inch (19mm) flat

Delta Ceramcoat Acrylic Paints

Dark Goldenrod   Tangerine   Calypso Orange   Purple Smoke   Avocado   Black Green   Light Ivory

Pumpkin   Poppy Orange   Black   Burnt Sienna   Payne's Grey

Enlarge or reduce this pattern to fit your project.

1 Prepare the Surface and Basecoat

Enlarge the pattern and cut the plywood in the shape of the scarecrow. Glue a wooden stake to the back and insert it into the ground. Seal your wood with wood sealer. When dry, lightly sand away the roughness and wipe clean. Apply the pattern using the black graphite paper and stylus.
Basecoat using your ³/₄-inch (19mm) flat and the following:

Hat: Dark Goldenrod
Face: Tangerine
Collar and cuffs: Calypso Orange
Shirt: Purple Smoke
Pants: Avocado
Shoes: Black Green
Hands: Light Ivory
Hat patches: Purple Smoke
Pants patches: Calypso Orange

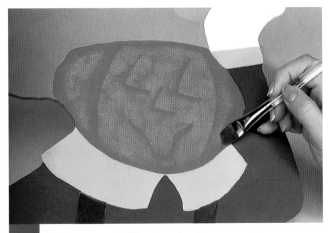

2 Sponge and Shade the Face

Using a damp sea sponge, pick up Pumpkin and sponge all over the head. Apply the pattern for the face detail using white graphite paper and a stylus.

Using a ⅝-inch (16mm) angle and Poppy Orange, shade along the outer edge of the head and to the outside of each section line. Float along the left and lower edge of the eye and nose cutout, and then under the mouth.

4 Detail the Face

Using your no. 1 liner and thinned Black, outline the eyes, nose and mouth. Be sure to line the top of the mouth and pull out nice smile lines. Use the handle of your brush to apply a Light Ivory dot in each eye.

3 Basecoat the Face

Use Calypso Orange and a no. 8 flat to basecoat the cut edge of the eyes, nose and mouth. Basecoat the rest of the eyes, nose and mouth with Black.

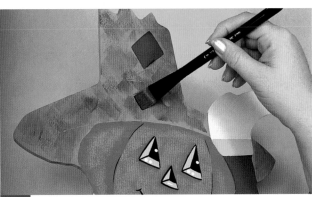

5 Paint the Straw Hat

Using your ¾-inch (19mm) brush, apply Burnt Sienna on the hat in all directions. Using a flat brush, stroke the paint on an angle to the right. The next stroke will angle to the left, making a loose X. Do this randomly over the entire area. It is okay to have the strokes overlap. Keep it loose with no definite pattern. This is known as the slip-slap method.

6 Shade and Highlight the Hat

With your ⅝-inch (16mm) angle and Burnt Sienna, shade above the hat brim, on either side of the hand, under the hat brim, and next to the head. Highlight with Calypso Orange along the brim's edge.

7 Shade the Collar and Cuffs

With your ⅝-inch (16mm) angle and Poppy Orange, shade under the head on the collar, and on the outside edges of the collar and cuffs.

8 Add Dots and Stripes

Add Purple Smoke dots to the collar, cuff and pants patch with the handle end of your brush. With your no. 1 liner and thinned Calypso Orange, line the shirt and patches vertically, then horizontally.

9 Shade the Shirt and Hands

With Payne's Grey and your ⅝-inch (16mm) angle brush, shade both sides of the shirt straps, under the collar, next to the cuffs, on the left arm next to his head, and on his right arm from the elbow back towards his armpit. Next, shade to the right of the center line and above his pants. With Avocado, float along the lower edge of his right hand and thumb. Shade the left hand along the left side.

10 Make the Denim

With a no. 8 fabric scrubber brush and Black Green, scrub his pants and straps.

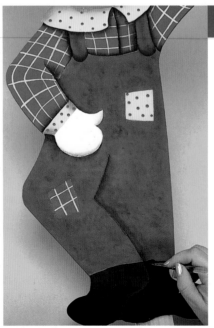

11 Add Final Shading

Still using Black Green, load the ⅝-inch (16mm) angle brush, and shade above and below his right arm. Then shade the straps under the collar and along the bottom of each one. Separate his legs by floating to the right of the line. Separate the shoe with a float of Avocado along the heel and bottom of his right foot.

Paint stitching lines
around each of the
patches with Black
and the liner brush.
Apply several coats of
your favorite water-based
varnish.

Resources

Manufacturers

Delta Technical Coatings
2550 Pellissier Place
Whittier, CA 90601-1505
(800) 423-4135
ww.deltacrafts.com

Kunin Felt
Foss Manufacturing
380 Lafayette Rd.
PO Box 5000
Hampton, NH 03843-5000
(603) 929-6100
kuninfelt@fossmfg.com

Royal & Langnickel Brush Mfg., Inc.
6707 Broadway
Merrillville, IN 46410
(800) 247-2211
www.royalbrush.com

Retailers in Canada

Crafts Canada
2745 Twenty-ninth St. NE
Calgary, Alberta T1Y 7B5

Folk Art Enterprises
P.O. Box 1088
Ridgetown, Ontario N0P 2C0
(888) 214-0062

MacPherson Craft Wholesale
83 Queen St. E.
P.O. Box 1870
St. Mary's, Ontario N4X 1C2
(519) 284-1741

Maureen McNaughton Enterprises
RR #2
Belwood, Ontario N0B 1J0
(519) 843-5648

Mercury Art & Craft Supershop
332 Wellington St.
London, Ontario N6C 4P7
(519) 434-1636

Town & Country Folk Art Supplies
93 Green Lane
Thornhill, Ontario L3T 6K6
(905) 882-0199

Retailers in the United Kingdom

Art Express
Index House
70 Burley Road
Leeds LS3 1JX
Tel: 0800 731 4185
www.artexpress.co.uk

Crafts World
No 8 North Street
Guildford
Surrey GU1 4AF
Tel: 07000 757070

Chroma Colour Products
Unit 5 Pilton Estate
Pitlake
Croydon CR0 3RA
Tel: 020 8688 1991
www.chromacolour.com

Green & Stone
259 King's Road
London SW3 5EL
Tel: 020 7352 0837
greenandstone@enterprise.net

Hobbycrafts
River Court
Southern Sector
Bournemouth International Airport
Christchurch
Dorset BH23 6SE
Tel: 0800 272387

Homecrafts Direct
P.O. Box 38
Leicester LE1 9BU
Tel: 0116 251 3139

Index

Celebrate your favorite holidays
with crafts from North Light Books!

Create classic holiday decorations that everyone will love! You'll find 14 simple painting projects inside, from Santa figures and Christmas card holders to tree ornaments and candy dishes. Each one includes easy-to-follow instructions, step-by-step photographs and simple designs that you can use on candles, fabric or glass.

ISBN 1-58180-237-4, paperback, 112 pages, #32012-K

Make your holidays brighter and more special by creating your very own floral décor! Cele Kahle shows you how to create a variety of gorgeous arrangements, swags, topiaries, wreaths and more. You'll create 19 projects in all, using silk foliage, berries, fruit and ribbon. Each one comes with step-by-step guidelines and beautiful full-color photos.

ISBN 1-58180-259-5, paperback, 128 pages, #32124-K

These 21 adorable projects perfectly capture the spirit of the seasons. Each one is easy to make and simple enough to be completed in a single sitting. From leprechauns, Easter eggs and spooky witches to Thanksgiving turkeys and a polar bear on skis, there's something for everyone-including kids! You'll also find guidelines for creating magnets, buttons and pins.

ISBN 1-58180-104-1, paperback, 128 pages, #31792-K

These 20 beautiful wreath projects are perfect for celebrating those special times of year. You'll find a range of sizes and styles, utilizing a variety of creative materials, including dried herbs, cinnamon sticks, silk flowers, Autumn leaves, Christmas candy and more. Clear, step-by-step instructions ensure beautiful, long lasting results every time!

ISBN 1-58180-239-0, paperback, 144 pages, #32015-K

These books and other fine North Light titles are available from your local art & craft retailer, bookstore, online supplier or by calling 1-800-448-0915.